SEA DISASTERS

ANN WEIL

◀◀◀ Disasters ▶▶▶

Air Disasters
Deadly Storms
Earthquakes
Environmental Disasters
Fires
Mountain Disasters
Sea Disasters
Space Disasters
Terrorism
Volcanoes

Development: Kent Publishing Services, Inc.
Design and Production: Signature Design Group, Inc.

SADDLEBACK PUBLISHING, INC.
Three Watson
Irvine, CA 92618-2767

E-Mail: info@sdlback.com
Website: www.sdlback.com

Photo Credits: cover, page 51, Bettmann/Corbis; page 23, Ralph White/Corbis; page 41, Patrick Ward/Corbis; page 60, AFP/Corbis; page 61, Reuters NewMedia/Corbis

ISBN 1-56254-660-0

Printed in the United States of America

1 2 3 4 5 6 08 07 06 05 04 03

TABLE OF CONTENTS

DATAFILE

TIMELINE

May 29, 1914

The *Empress of Ireland* and the *Storstad* collide on the St. Lawrence River.

July 24, 1915

The *Eastland* steamship flips over on the Chicago River.

Where is the St. Lawrence River? ▶▶▶

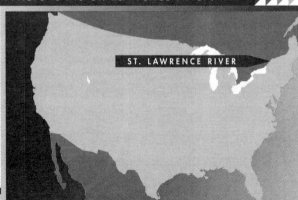

ST. LAWRENCE RIVER

DID YOU KNOW?

The *Storstad* was a ship from Norway. The front of the *Storstad* was built to be stronger than ice. When it collided with the *Empress of Ireland*, the *Storstad* stayed afloat.

KEY TERMS

steamship - a large boat powered by steam

reef - rock or sand near the surface of the water

captain - the person in charge of a ship

Chapter One:
Introduction

People built boats long before there were cars or trains or planes. People used boats to get from one place to another. Traveling over water was often easier than traveling over land.

Some ancient people used boats for fishing as well as traveling. Later, boats were used for trade. These boats traveled long distances. They brought back spices and other wonderful things from far away.

Explorers traveled by boat to see other parts of the world.

Steamships

In the 1600s, people in Europe were looking for new places to live. Some wanted to go to America. Others were bound for Australia. They built ships to carry a lot of people at once.

In the 1800s, steamships started replacing sailing ships. The new ships could go faster. More and more people traveled by ship. Accidents at sea claimed more and more lives.

Bad weather caused many shipwrecks. Fog and storms were often to blame. Some ships hit underwater reefs.

The people who built ships tried to make them safe. Sometimes, though, they made mistakes. Some shipwrecks were the result of poor design.

Captains also made mistakes. The captain is in charge of the ship.

A captain's decision at sea can mean life or death for the people on board. Some shipwrecks happened because the captain made a bad choice.

Many ships were sunk during the first and second World Wars. Some of these ships were carrying guns and soldiers. Others had ordinary people and families on board.

Some disasters at sea don't kill people. Oil spills pollute oceans and beaches. They kill birds and other animals. These disasters ruin our environment.

Eastland, Chicago River, 1915

This disaster happened on the morning of July 24, 1915. A steamship called the *Eastland* was docked on the Chicago River. It had been hired to take people to a company picnic. It was a big event.

The *Eastland* was supposed to be able to hold 2,500 people. However, more than that number got on board. The *Eastland* started to tip over. It was still tied to its dock on the Chicago River.

The ship rocked dangerously from side to side. Some of the crew jumped onto the dock. They saved themselves. Others on board were not so lucky.

The *Eastland* rolled over onto its side. It sank next to the dock. Many of the passengers ended up in the river. The ship was almost all covered with water.

Workers near the dock saw what happened. They threw wood into the water. Some people grabbed onto the wood. It helped them stay afloat.

Some people were trapped inside the ship. One worker cut a hole in the side of the ship. Forty people got out that way.

About 850 people drowned. The ship's bad design was to blame. The *Eastland* was top heavy. It could not hold steady with so many people on board.

People in charge of the *Eastland* should have corrected the problem. Others paid for the mistake with their lives.

TIMELINE

April 14, 1912
The *Titanic* crashes into an iceberg and begins to sink.

July 25, 1956
The *Andrea Doria* collides with the *Stockholm* off Nantucket Island, Massachusetts.

Where did the Titanic sink?

TITANIC SUNK

DID YOU KNOW?

The passengers aboard the *Titanic* had rooms based on their social class. The rich lived on the top level. The poor lived on the lowest level, making it hard for them to escape.

KEY TERMS

ocean liner - a ship carrying passengers

lifeboat - a small boat carried by a ship for use if the ship begins to sink

crow's nest - a look-out position on the front of a ship

funnel - the smokestack of a steamship

Chapter Two:
Titanic, 1912

The *Titanic* is one of the most famous shipwrecks in history. There are many books and movies about the *Titanic*. They all tell the well-known story of the ship's first trip across the Atlantic–a trip that ended in disaster.

In 1912, the *Titanic* was the biggest moving object ever built. The ship was four city blocks long. It was as high as an 11-story building.

The people who built the *Titanic* made it beautiful as well as big. They thought they had made it safe as well.

The *Titanic* was called "unsinkable." Maybe that's why the owners ignored something very important. There were not enough lifeboats for all the passengers. That was a tragic mistake.

A Close Call

The *Titanic* left Southampton, England, on April 10, 1912. The ship was on its way to America. This was its first trip across the Atlantic. It did not begin well. The *Titanic* almost collided with another large ocean liner.

As it left, the *Titanic* passed another ocean liner tied to the dock. This ocean liner was called the *New York*.

The *New York* broke loose from its ropes. It drifted toward the *Titanic*. The captain of the *Titanic* saw what was happening. He quickly turned away from the *New York*. The two ships missed each other by only a few feet.

That accident was avoided. But a worse accident was yet to come. It would have deadly results for those aboard the *Titanic*.

"Iceberg, right ahead!"

Four days after leaving England, the *Titanic* was speeding through the north Atlantic. There were reports from other ships that there was a lot of ice nearby. Another captain might have slowed the *Titanic* down. However, Captain Smith kept the *Titanic* moving at full speed. He wanted to set a new record for crossing the Atlantic. The owners hoped that it would be good for business.

One of the crew was high up in the ship's crow's nest. His job was to watch out for ice. At 11:40 at night on April 14, 1912, he saw something terrifying. A huge iceberg was in front of the ship. He rang the warning bell three times.

The person steering the boat reacted right away. He tried to avoid the iceberg. However, it's not easy to turn a huge ship quickly.

For more than 30 seconds, nothing happened. It looked as though the *Titanic* would hit the iceberg head on.

Then the *Titanic* started to turn away from the iceberg. But it was too little, too late. The *Titanic* bumped into the iceberg. The sharp ice scraped against the *Titanic*. Water poured into the front of the ship. Captain Smith used the radio to call for help. Another ocean liner answered right away. The *Carpathia* was more than 60 miles away.

Captain Smith knew it would take the *Carpathia* four hours traveling at its top speed to reach the sinking *Titanic*. He knew the *Titanic* would be underwater by then. He also knew there was only enough room in the lifeboats for about half the people on board.

"Women and children first!"

The first lifeboat was launched about an hour after the ship hit the iceberg. It had room for 65 people. There were only 28 inside.

The *Titanic* was tilting lower into the water. It was obvious now that the great ship was truly sinking. More and more people crowded in the lifeboats. Women and children went first. Some men jumped into lifeboats to save themselves. They knew there was no hope of surviving unless they did.

It was clear that not everyone would fit in the lifeboats. Still, more people could have been saved if the crew had known what to do and acted more quickly. Two lifeboats were not even used. They were washed off the deck as the *Titanic* sank.

Lights Out for the *Titanic*

The front of the *Titanic* was the first part to go under. Some people moved up to higher parts of the ship. Others went overboard.

One of the tall smoke stacks on top of the ship fell over. It crushed many people fighting for their lives in the icy water.

Exactly what happened that night is still a mystery. Survivors had their own stories to tell. Some people reported that they saw the ship break in half. Others said they saw the whole ship sink in one piece. The lights of the ship went out as it disappeared underwater.

705 Rescued

About 1,500 people ended up in the icy water. Most of the lifeboats had already moved away from the ship. They did not want to get sucked underwater as the *Titanic* sank.

Some of the boats still had room for more people. But most of the people in the lifeboats were afraid to go back and save others. They thought the people in the water would rush the lifeboats and tip them over. Instead, they tried to block out the cries for help.

Only one lifeboat actually returned to look for survivors. Five more people were saved this way. The rest were left to slowly freeze to death and drown. Some of them were rich and famous Americans. Others were poor people with dreams of a better life for themselves and their children in America.

Finally, the *Carpathia* arrived. It was too late to save those in the water. But the ship did rescue the lucky ones who had made it into the lifeboats. Of the more than 2,000 who left England five days ago, only 705 survived. Captain Smith had gone down with his ship.

Finding the Wreck

The *Titanic* sank to the bottom of the ocean. People still had many questions about what happened that night in 1912. The answers lay with the ship more than 2 miles underwater.

The *Titanic* was found on the bottom of the ocean in 1985. A small submarine took scientists down to where the *Titanic* was resting on the ocean floor. They used special equipment to light and photograph what remained of the great ship. They discovered that the damage to the ship was much less than originally thought.

People had thought that the iceberg had cut a long gash in the side of the ship. They assumed the damage must have been great to sink the unsinkable *Titanic.* Instead, they found a few small holes in the side of the ship. They also saw how the ice crumpled some of the metal plates on the ship's hull.

The wreck was in two pieces. Some survivors reported seeing the ship break into two before it sank. Still, the ship might have broken as it made its way down through the water.

Finding the wreck answered some of the questions people had about the *Titanic.* But some of the mystery still remains.

The wreck of the Titanic *was found on the bottom of the ocean in 1985.*

Andrea Doria, 1956

Andrea Doria was an Italian cruise ship. It was safer than the *Titanic*. There had been many changes since that disaster.

On July 25, 1956, *Andrea Doria* was off Nantucket Island, Massachusetts. There was a thick fog. It was hard to see far.

Andrea Doria's radar showed that there was another ship nearby. The captain tried to avoid the other ship. The other ship also tried to avoid the *Andrea Doria*. Both ships turned. But instead of avoiding each other, the two ships collided.

The other ship was a Swedish ocean liner named *Stockholm*. *Stockholm* punched a hole in the side of the Italian ship. The hole was about thirty feet deep.

Water rushed in. The ship tilted over onto one side. That side was too low in the water to launch the lifeboats.

The captain of the *Andrea Doria* used the radio to call for help. A French ocean liner came to the rescue. It picked up survivors and brought them to shore.

52 people died in that accident. The ship sank the next morning.

TIMELINE

June 15, 1904
A fire breaks out on the *General Slocum*.

February 16, 1993
A storm strikes the *Neptune*, a ferry carrying more than 1,000 people in Haiti.

Where is Haiti?

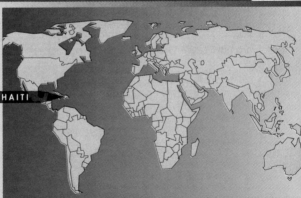

DID YOU KNOW?

When the storm hit the *Neptune*, people panicked. Many people crowded onto the top deck. Their weight caused the deck to crash down.

KEY TERMS

ferry - a boat used to take people or things across a river or bay

lifejacket - a device that a person can wear to keep from drowning

aground - onto the shore or the bottom of a river, lake, etc.

Chapter Three:
Ferry Disasters

Ferries carry people across a river or other body of water. Some ferries travel only a very short distance. Others go out into the open sea and cross many miles of rough water.

People all over the world use ferries. Ferries are often the fastest and least expensive way to get from one place to another.

Modern-day ferries carry thousands of people at a time. A ferry accident can cost thousands of lives. These are some of the worst disasters at sea.

General Slocum, New York City, June 1904

The *General Slocum* disaster was a horrible tragedy. More than 1,000 people died when the ferry caught fire. Many of the victims were children. They and their families were going to a church picnic.

On June 15, 1904, about 1,300 people boarded the *General Slocum*. At about 9:30, the ferry left from a dock on the East River in New York City. The *General Slocum* was supposed to take the church group to Huntington, Long Island for the picnic. But it didn't work out that way.

The ferry steamed up the East River. Children played on the deck and watched the other boats in the river. A band was playing. The adults talked and listened to the music.

Fire!

Then disaster struck. People started yelling "Fire!" The crew tried to put it out. They pulled out the fire hoses. But the hoses had rotted away. They were useless. The hoses burst when the water was turned on.

The fire spread quickly. The front of the ship was in flames. People panicked. Children and their parents were terrified. They ran to the back of the ship.

The captain kept the ship moving at full speed. He wanted to get to land quickly. Then the people could get off the burning ship. However, there were many oil tanks on the docks. He could not land near them. The fire from the ship would cause an explosion. He decided to head for North Brother Island. There were no oil tanks there. But the island was a mile away.

The captain's clothes were on fire as he steered the ship. The wind fanned the flames. The fire took over more of the ferry. The flames moved toward men, women, and children crowded in the back of the boat.

Everyone was terrified. Children were crying. Their parents were screaming. Most of the people on board could not swim. Some of them put on lifejackets. But the lifejackets were old. The filling inside had rotted. They were as useless as the broken fire hoses.

The crew could not lower the lifeboats. The boats were wired in place. The crew could not get them loose. Besides, the ship was going too fast. It was impossible to safely lower the lifeboats. By the time the ship stopped, the lifeboats had already burned.

Hospital Rescue

The ship ran aground at North Brother Island. By then it was almost completely destroyed by the fire. There was a hospital on the island. Nurses and patients rushed to help the survivors. They brought ladders so people could climb down from the burning ship. Parents threw their children overboard. They hoped the people below would catch them.

The patients inside watched the scene in horror. People were burning to death. Others were drowning in the deep water. Some were pulled from the water. They were the lucky few. Most of the people on the *General Slocum* that day were not saved. 1,021 of the 1,358 on board died.

Neptune, Haiti, 1993

Haiti is in the Caribbean. It is a poor country. The roads are bad. There are not a lot of cars or buses.

Many Haitians use ferries. It is the only way to get to some places on their island. Most of the ferries are small. They are old. They break down. Many of them are not safe.

Sometimes, too many people crowd onto a ferry. This overcrowding causes some ferry accidents.

The worst Haitian ferry accident happened in 1993. The *Neptune* was on its way from Jeremie to Port-au-Prince. Port-au-Prince is Haiti's largest city. It usually took 12 hours to make the 150-mile trip.

The ferry was very crowded. More than a thousand people squeezed onto it. The ferry also carried animals and lots of charcoal.

There was a storm. The wind and waves rocked the ferry. People began to panic. Some rushed to one side of the ferry. Others crowded on the top deck.

The weight of all those people was too much. The deck caved in. It crashed down onto hundreds of people below. Then the ferry tipped over.

There were no lifejackets. People grabbed whatever they could to help stay afloat. Some people survived by holding onto the bodies of dead cows. But most of the people drowned.

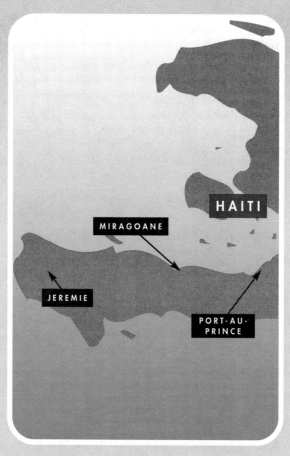

The triple-deck ship ran into a heavy
rainstorm about halfway through the voyage
and went down near the coastal town of
Miragoane.

Estonia, Baltic Sea, 1994

The *Estonia* was traveling from Tallinn,

Estonia to Stockholm, Sweden. It had

almost 1,000 people on board. The

weather was bad. A storm rocked the

huge ferry. One of the doors was thrown

open. Water rushed into the ship.

The ferry started to tip over. At first the

crew did not know what was going on.

They saw the ferry was leaning over. But

they didn't know why. They turned the

ship into the waves. They hoped the force

of the water would push the ferry back

upright. But the opposite happened. More water poured in through the open door. Then the *Estonia* rolled over.

Most of the people on board were trapped. They tried to get up to the decks. But it was difficult for them to escape.

The *Estonia* sank on September 28, 1994. Most of the people on board that day died. There were only 137 survivors.

DATAFILE

TIMELINE

December 26, 1998
A storm threatens sailors in the Sydney to Hobart race.

January 1, 1999
Floral wreaths are dropped into the water in memory of the sailors who died in the storm.

Where is Sydney?

SYDNEY

DID YOU KNOW?

The storm during the Sydney to Hobart race caused waves to rise as high as 50 feet. The water tossed the boats around like bathtub toys.

KEY TERMS

Boxing Day - a holiday celebrated the day after Christmas in the United Kingdom, Canada, and Australia

skipper - the captain of a boat

capsize - to overturn

Chapter Four:
Sydney to Hobart

Sailing is a very popular sport. Millions of people all over the world sail boats for fun. Racing is an exciting way to test a sailor's skill.

Racing sailboats are built for speed and safety. They are made to sail through storms. A good boat with a clever crew can handle most storms.

However, the storm that hit the Sydney to Hobart race in 1998 was not like other bad storms. This was the worst storm to ever strike the race.

The storm turned the Sydney to Hobart race into a fight for survival. It was no longer about who would win. It was about who would finish alive.

Sailboats in Sydney Harbor at the start of the Sydney to Hobart race in New South Wales, Australia.

December 26, 1998

The day after Christmas is called Boxing Day. In Australia, Boxing Day is well-known as the start of their biggest sailing race, the Sydney to Hobart.

On Boxing Day 1998, more than a hundred boats were ready to race. They were lined up in Sydney harbor. At 1 P.M., a cannon signaled the race had begun. The 54th Sydney to Hobart race was underway.

However, the weather reports were not good. A storm was predicted. That evening some of the boat crews saw lightning. It lit up the sky. The waves got bigger.

December 27, 1998

On the second day of the race, some of the boats stopped racing. They were afraid the storm would destroy their boat. Other boats stayed in the race. Some were already very far from shore. They could not make it back easily.

The water was very rough. Many sailors were seasick. They could not help sail their boats.

The waves got even bigger. Some were as tall as a six-story building. They looked like snow-capped mountains.

Rescue by Helicopter

A monster wave crashed onto the boat *Stand Aside*. It ripped off the roof of the cabin. Some of the crew were badly hurt. One sailor lost part of a finger. Others had bad cuts. The boat was full of water. It was sinking.

A TV helicopter was taking pictures of the race. The pilot saw what happened. He radioed for help. A rescue helicopter arrived. It had the equipment to pull people up out of the water.

The helicopter crew had a difficult and dangerous job. The pilot had to keep the helicopter steady in storm winds. One of the crew was lowered down to the water on a rope. The survivors were bobbing up and down in the fifty-foot waves.

The first helicopter got eight of the crew safely up and out. A second helicopter rescued the remaining four.

The first rescue by helicopter was a success. However, more boats needed help. Many sailors were badly hurt when waves flung their boats around.

Altogether, helicopters whisked more than 50 sailors to safety. Still, they could not save everyone.

Buried at Sea

The storm turned deadly. The roar of the wind was deafening. The rain came down so hard it stung the skin and blinded the eyes.

The crew of *Sword of Orion* decided to quit the race. They changed course. However, their decision to turn back came too late to save one of their crew.

A huge wave banged into the boat. *Sword of Orion* slid down the wave. Part of the boat was underwater. One of the crew was knocked overboard. His name was Glyn Charles. The boat was moving away from him fast.

Another sailor wanted to jump in after Charles. He was stopped before he could jump into the water. It was hopeless. Charles disappeared from sight. His body was never found.

Two More Dead

Like other boats in the race, *Business Post Naiad* was in trouble. A monster wave flipped the boat. Some of the crew was trapped underwater. A couple minutes later, another enormous wave spun the boat back upright. By then one of the crew had already drowned. The skipper had a heart attack and died.

It was a terrifying night for the rest of the crew of the *Business Post Naiad.* The next morning, a helicopter came to rescue the seven survivors.

Business Post Naiad was eventually towed to shore with the bodies of the two dead men on board.

Life and Death in a Lifeboat

The nine-man crew of the *Winston Churchill* had abandoned their boat. They were crowded into two life rafts.

The storm hurled the small lifeboats up and down. A huge wave capsized one of the rafts. Two of the men inside managed to hold on. But the other three tumbled into the water.

The two survivors were rescued. So were the four men in the other raft. Rescue planes searched for the missing three. But they were lost at sea.

January 1, 1999

Six floral wreaths were dropped from a dock in Hobart. They were in memory of the six sailors who died during the Sydney to Hobart race. The storm could have taken more. Search and rescue teams on the water and in the air risked their lives to save others. They were the heroes of the disaster.

TIMELINE

May 7, 1915
A German submarine fires a torpedo at the
Lusitania, a British ocean liner.

August 12, 2000
An explosion rips through the Russian
submarine, *Kursk*.

Where is Russia? ▶▶▶

DID YOU KNOW?

64 bodies were found right after the *Kursk* disaster. Divers looked for more bodies, but it was getting too dangerous. They couldn't get into parts of the submarine without hurting themselves.

KEY TERMS

torpedo - a large missile which moves underwater to destroy enemy ships

battleship - a big warship covered in armor and carrying guns

submarine - a ship that travels underwater

Chapter Five:
War and Military

Traveling during a war is risky. Countries at war try to sink each other's ships. Some of the worst disasters at sea happened during war time.

Lusitania, 1915

The *Lusitania* was a British ocean liner. It left New York City on May 1, 1915. The ship was going to England.

In 1915, the world was at war. German submarines were sinking British ships. The German government sent out a warning. They said that people should not travel on British ships.

The German government put a notice in one of the New York newspapers. It said that people traveling into a war zone were at risk. This notice appeared the same morning the *Lusitania* left New York City. It was a deadly coincidence.

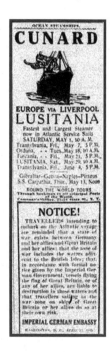

Newspaper ad warning people about traveling in a war zone.

On May 7, 1915, a German submarine fired a torpedo at the *Lusitania*. It was on target. A lookout on the *Lusitania* saw the torpedo coming. But there was nothing the crew could do.

The torpedo hit the ship. There was a large explosion. Fires broke out. The grand ocean liner sank in less than 20 minutes. About 1,200 of the almost 2,000 people on board were killed.

Bismarck, May 1941

The *Bismarck* was a World War II German battleship. It had a crew of about 2,300 soldiers.

The *Bismarck* fought in the Battle of the Denmark Strait. A British warship sank during that battle. The *Bismarck* survived the battle. But it needed some repairs. The ship headed toward France. It could be fixed there.

On the way, other British battleships attacked it. It took the British less than two hours to sink the *Bismarck*. Only 110 of her crew survived.

Thresher, 1963

Thresher was deep underwater near Cape Cod, Massachusetts when something went wrong. The submarine lost all power. It sank deeper and deeper. Then it broke apart. The force of the water crushed the submarine. All 129 men on the submarine died.

The men on the submarine were still alive as it began to sink. They must have heard the submarine start to break apart. Then it was only seconds before they were dead.

Wilhelm Gustloff, 1945

The *Wilhelm Gustloff* was a German ocean liner. It left Danzig, Germany, in January, 1945. (Danzig is now Gdansk, Poland.) There were 6,000 to 10,000 people on board.

Germany and Russia were enemies during World War II. A Russian submarine fired a torpedo at the German liner. It sank the ship. Only 1,000 people survived. This was the single most deadly shipwreck in history.

Kursk, 2000

A Russian submarine sank with 118 on board. 23 of them were still alive when the submarine hit the bottom. They waited to be rescued. But help came too late. None of the crew survived the disaster.

Special listening equipment recorded two explosions near where the Kursk went down. What caused these explosions is still not known. One possibility is that fuel caught fire. The fire caused the torpedoes to explode.

TIMELINE

January 16, 2001
An oil tanker hits the Galapagos Islands, spilling almost 200,000 gallons of fuel.

November 19, 2002
The *Prestige* oil tanker cracks and begins to leak oil into the water.

Where did the *Prestige* oil spill occur? ▶▶▶

COAST OF SPAIN

DID YOU KNOW?

There are more than 2,000 tankers in U.S. waters. These tankers must follow strict safety laws. The United States wants to protect the environment and people from the damage of an oil spill.

KEY TERMS

oil tanker - a ship with big tanks for carrying oil

sturdy - strong, built to last

tortoise - a turtle, usually a turtle which lives on land

Chapter Six:
Prestige Oil Spill

The *Prestige* was an old oil tanker. On November 19, 2002, the ship was hit by a bad storm. It was off the coast of Spain. The force of the storm caused the *Prestige* to crack. A lot of oil poured into the sea.

The *Prestige* was built more than 26 years ago. Newer oil tankers are better built and safer. However, the *Prestige* was not very sturdy. The force of the storm broke the ship into two pieces. Then it sank.

A lot of oil was still inside the ship when it sank. This oil leaked out.

The oil polluted the water. Thick,

black oil washed up on shore. It is very difficult to clean up after an oil spill. The oil spreads over a large area.

That part of Spain was famous for its shellfish and octopus. Many villages depended on the sea. Now, people could not fish there. They had no other way to make a living.

The oil killed birds as well as fish and shellfish. Many of these birds were rare.

Workers patched up some of the underwater holes in the ship. This stopped the oil leaking out. But it did not solve the problem. A sunken ship rots away over time. The metal rusts. More holes will appear. And more oil will leak out.

Oil may continue to leak from the *Prestige* for years.

Jessica, 2001

The Galapagos Islands are famous for
their giant tortoises. Many rare animals
live on these isolated islands. In January
2001, a tanker ran aground on one of
the islands. Oil leaked from the ship.
It was one of the worst disasters to hit
the Galapagos.

Volunteers clean up oil from the 2001 oil spill.

The ship *Jessica* was carrying 160,000 gallons of diesel fuel and about 80,000 gallons of other liquids when it ran aground near the Galapagos Islands. The spill affected animals including sea lions and pelicans. Volunteers were on standby to clean up and rescue them.

Epilogue

The U.S. Coast Guard (USCG) is a branch of the military. The USCG protects people in the country's ports and waterways, along the coast, and even on international waters. It also protects the environment and the country's economic interests in these areas.

The USCG has a search and rescue program. When in danger, a person can make a distress call to the USCG. A search and rescue unit aims to be ready within 30 minutes of the call. Each day the Coast Guard helps about 192 people in distress.

One of the program goals is to save at least 93 percent of people in danger of dying. Each day, the Coast Guard saves about 10 lives.

Bibliography

Alcraft, Rob. *Oil Disasters*. World's Worst. Des Plaines, IL: Heinemann Library, 2000.

Delgado, James P. *Wrecks of American Warships*. Watts Library. New York: Franklin Watts, 2000.

Harmon, Daniel E. *The Titanic.* Great Disasters, Reforms and Ramifications. Philadelphia: Chelsea House Publishers, 2001.

Higgins, Chris. *Nuclear Submarine Disasters*. Great Disasters, Reforms and Ramifications. Philadelphia: Chelsea House Publishers, 2002.

Landau, Elaine. *Maritime Disasters*. Watts Library. New York: Franklin Watts, 1999.

Index